GREEN ARRO

AND THE LNER V2 CLASS

by

Michael Rutherford and Michael Blakemore

Pioneer V2 No.4771 Green Arrow *with a down express freight near Potters Bar in 1937. During that year King's Cross V2s were allocated to regular crews in No.3 Link and* Green Arrow *went to Driver J. Burgess.*
(NRM/P. Ransome-Wallis 1988)

Published by Atlantic Transport Publishers,
Trevithick House, West End, Penryn, Cornwall, TR10 8HE
in association with
The Friends of the National Railway Museum,
Leeman Road, York, YO2 4XJ

First published 1997
© Michael Rutherford and Michael Blakemore, 1997
ISBN: 0 906899 77 X
Design and layout: Barry C. Lane, Sutton-in-Craven
Reproduction and printing by The Amadeus Press Ltd,
Huddersfield, West Yorkshire

British Cataloguing in Publication Data
A catalogue record for this book is available
from the British Library

DESIGN AND THE DESIGNER

New locomotive designs are often presented, particularly by enthusiasts, as the products of intellectual genius rather than of drawing offices and workshops. They are presented as a solution demanding a problem and thus the operating department takes the new machine and draws up improved services around it. Whilst this impression may contain *some* grains of truth with regard to early and mid-Victorian Britain and certain railway companies, in general — and certainly in this century — new locomotive designs were prepared in order for the operating department to fulfil its own plans for improved services, plans often resulting from competitive commercial considerations and customer demands.

The reasons for this misconception centre around the position of the locomotive superintendent (later, chief mechanical engineer) of the larger railway companies in Britain who was responsible for the maintenance of a suitable stock of locomotives to work the companies' services and who was answerable directly to the board of directors. A sub-committee of the latter usually discussed the supply of new and replacement locomotives and approved the spending of appropriate monies (usually based on estimates). In most other parts of the world locomotives have been supplied by private manufacturers and 'designed' by a mix of the manufacturers' own design departments, consulting engineers and the railway company's staff in varying proportions.

From the very early years of the railways in Britain, many of the larger companies began to design and then build their own locomotives and this became the norm. It also altered the status of the locomotive superintendent somewhat as he became closely associated with his company's locomotives and became a public figure — railway locomotives were one of the main subjects of interest to a public attracted to machines and 'progress'.

As the complexity of managing a large railway company increased, the mechanical engineering department, with its high budget, became of increased concern to railway management as a whole and gradually the officer in charge became a senior member of the management team, subordinate to the general manager, rather than a loose cannon answerable only to the board. While locomotive (and carriage and wagon) design continued to be of no less importance than previously, in many cases the increasing amounts of administration requiring supervision by the chief mechanical engineer saw him delegating a great deal of his design functions to his chief draughtsman and the drawing office staff.

Nigel Gresley (as he then was) with his two daughters on the footplate of the high-pressure 4-6-4 'Hush-Hush' at a press demonstration at King's Cross on 8th January 1930. (NRM 3609/76)

Before the advent of Green Arrow *and the V2s, K3 2-6-0 No.153 (in shiny LNER black livery) heads the down 'Scotch Goods' past Cemetery box, New Southgate, in 1932.* (NRM/LPC 23876)

This was particularly the case on the railways of Britain after the Grouping of 1923, except for Nigel (later Sir Nigel) Gresley of the London & North Eastern Railway. Because of the parlous state of that new conglomerate's finances in the 1920s, it was decided not to undertake any major corporate restructuring or rationalization and standardization and the previous constituent companies were held together in a loose federation with a good deal of autonomy given to the mechanical engineers in charge of their own areas and workshops. This state of affairs gave Gresley the opportunity to involve himself much more closely with new locomotive designs and to stamp his own personal mark on them.

This 'hands-on' approach led to both idiosyncrasies and genuine progress in locomotive engineering and by the late 1930s Sir Nigel (he was knighted in 1936) had raised the status of locomotive engineering in Britain back to its Victorian pre-eminence and was one of its most respected practitioners on a worldwide stage.

Herbert Nigel Gresley was born on 19th June 1876, the fifth child of the Reverend Nigel Gresley, rector of Netherseale in Derbyshire. In 1893 he obtained a premium apprenticeship at the Crewe Works of the London & North Western Railway under the formidable F.W. Webb and stayed on for an extra year in the works to gain more practical experience. He then became a pupil under J.A.F. (later Sir John) Aspinall at the Horwich Works of the Lancashire & Yorkshire Railway where he gained valuable drawing office experience and spent some time in charge of the materials test room. After this he became foreman of the locomotive running sheds at Blackpool where a 'feel' for the running side of locomotive matters was acquired that would have been unobtainable from a textbook; managing Blackpool depot could be a particularly difficult task during the summer holiday period.

From 1900 to 1911 Gresley was away from locomotives and involved with carriage and wagon work, firstly on the LYR (where he was rapidly promoted) and then on the Great Northern Railway where in March 1905, at the remarkably young age of 29, he became C&W Superintendent under H.A. Ivatt, the Locomotive Superintendent. When the latter retired at the end of September 1911, Gresley was appointed as his replacement.

Very many of the foundations of Sir Nigel's later 'big engine' policy had already been laid by Ivatt — his wide firebox Atlantics, a proposal (in 1907) for a mixed traffic 2-6-2 locomotive using the aforementioned Atlantic's boiler and multi-cylinder designs for fast main line running. The enhanced services required by passengers (catering facilities, heating, electric lighting and greater comfort) in the new century saw train weights rise and the demand for faster timings meant that more powerful locomotives were essential.

Similar requirements arose on the freight side, particularly with regard to the increasing supply of fresh food such as fish, meat and seasonal vegetables. The expanding region in and around London had an insatiable demand for such produce and the GNR (and later the LNER) was in an excellent position to provide transport for Scottish meat, east coast fish and a whole

The V2s evolved out of plans for an enlarged K3 class 2-6-0, 193 of which were built between 1920 and 1937. No.61912, pictured here at Doncaster in 1956, was built in May 1931 by Armstrong, Whitworth & Co. as LNER No.1141 and was withdrawn from service in September 1962. (M. Rutherford collection)

range of vegetables from Lincolnshire and East Anglia. There were also demands from traders to introduce faster goods services between the major cities. At first valuable loads and perishables were sent in vans attached to passenger trains but gradually new services of fast freight trains were introduced, either wholly or partially fitted with continuous brakes.

The earliest locomotives designed for this sort of traffic were large-wheeled inside-cylinder superheated 0-6-0s and Gresley provided some himself from 1911. He later introduced 2-6-0s with outside cylinders and valve gear (making preparation and maintenance easier), piston valves and superheaters. Larger-boilered examples were introduced and in March 1920 came No.1000, the first of his three-cylinder 2-6-0s (LNER Class K3). This prototype followed various wartime preparations for some railway standard locomotives and most proposals included boilers of 6ft in diameter. No.1000 incorporated this feature and also the first application of Gresley's famous 2-to-1 conjugated valve gear, although he had previously built a heavy freight 2-8-0 with three cylinders and a different design of conjugated valve gear (No.461 in 1918).

Two ex-North Eastern Railway Class Z (LNER C7) three-cylinder Atlantics were rebuilt with boosters which were carried in a bogie which articulated the locomotive to the tender. No.2171 of this Class C9 is shown here at Haymarket (Edinburgh) in August 1932. It was proposed to articulate a large-wheeled K3 in this manner (but without the booster). (Photomatic 6455)

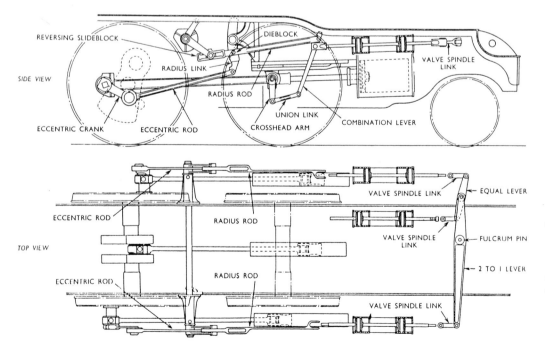

Gresley's patent 2-to-1 derived valve gear as fitted to his three-cylinder engines and used by a number of railways, throughout every continent. It was controversial in that when badly maintained, the events of the middle valve could be very erratic. When the levers were mounted behind the cylinders (as in the D49 class 4-4-0s) no problems occurred but when mounted as shown, char and grit from the cleaning of the smokebox found its way into the fulcrum pin where, mixed with grease, it formed a very effective grinding paste. Lack of maintenance during the war and post-war years affected V2 performance in particular but when the engines were properly serviced the problems were minimal.

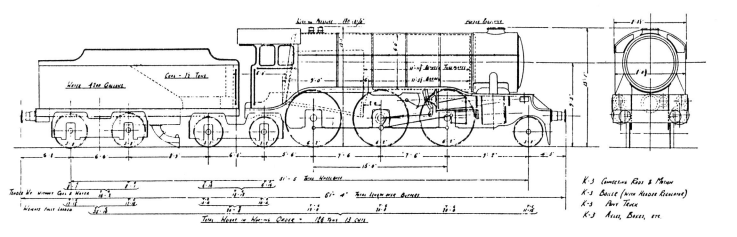

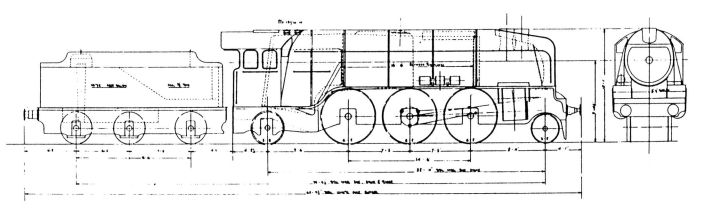

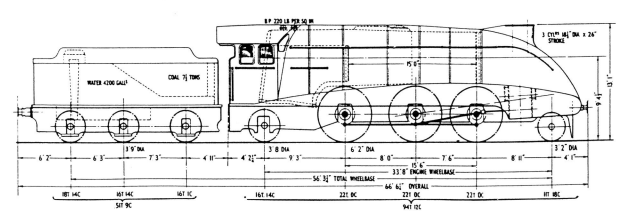

Concurrently Gresley had been working on the design of a new large express passenger locomotive, evolving on paper from a four-cylinder Pacific (in 1915) and then to a three-cylinder 2-6-2 before finally settling on a three-cylinder Pacific (both in 1918). It was some years before a final design was drawn up in detail but the first 4-6-2, Class A1 No.1470 *Great Northern,* entered traffic in April 1922. Between that time and 1925 a total of 52 were constructed. Although more powerful than earlier locomotives on the East Coast Main Line (this was only to be expected in view of their much increased size), they were not, however, greatly more efficient and could be quite heavy on coal. An improved design, the A3 class, was developed by modifying two existing A1s (Nos.2544 *Lemberg* and 4480 *Enterprise*) in 1927; higher-pressure boilers were fit-

The three earlier schemes before Green Arrow: *(top) the 6ft 2in 'Improved K3' with articulated connection to the tender, (middle) the first V2 outline, a mini-*Cock o' the North *complete with rotary cam poppet valve gear, ACFI feedwater heater and double Kylchap exhaust, and (bottom) a streamlined version of 1935 based on the A4 then under construction but still including a double Kylchap exhaust, a feature not built into the A4 design until the 28th engine of the class, No.4468* Mallard, *in March 1938.*

ted and valve gear and valves modified to give improved performance. These results were so promising that more improvements were incorporated by the drawing office (such as redesigned frames) and 27 new A3s were built between 1928 and 1935, older A1s being duly converted to A3s as they passed through Doncaster Works for heavy repairs.

TABLE 1 — Fast Freight Locomotives GNR & LNER

Class GN	LNE	Date introduced	Type	Driving wheel diameter ft	in	Cylinders dia in	stroke in	Position	Max boiler diameter ft	in	Grate area sq ft	Boiler pressure	Tractive effort at 85% BP lbs	Engine weight in working order ton	cwt	Notes
J21	J2	1912	0-6-0	5	8	19 × 26		2 inside	4	8	19.0	170	19,945	50	10	Superheated version
H2	K1	1912	2-6-0	5	8	20 × 26		2 outside	4	8	24.5	170 (later 180)	22,100 (later 23,400)	61	14	All rebuilt to K2
H3	K2	1914	2-6-0	5	8	20 × 26		2 outside	5	6	24.0	170 (later 180)	22,100 (later 23,400)	63	14	Later batches heavier
H4	K3	1920	2-6-0	5	8	18½ × 26		3	6	0	28.0	180	30,031	71	14	Some batches heavier
—	V2ʼ	1936	2-6-2	6	2	18½ × 26		3	6	5	41.25	220	33,730	93	2	

In the meantime further K3 three-cylinder 2-6-0s had been built, 60 in 1924/5 and 49 in 1929-31. Whilst they were admirable engines and could run at speeds up to 80mph, the K3s rode very roughly at speed and were colloquially known to footplatemen as 'Jazzers'. New fast freight services were being developed to give guaranteed city-to-city deliveries to traders; these seem to have originated with the Great Western Railway and a scheme it tagged the 'Green Arrow' service, although there was soon a certain amount of co-operation between the companies in this field.

Gresley, in discussions with his subordinate area mechanical engineers and also with the locomotive running department (for which he was not responsible — that being the prerogative of the Chief General Manager through his own subordinates), decided that a larger-wheeled (6ft 2in) 'improved' K3 was required and in order to stabilize the riding at speed it was proposed to articulate the tender to the rear of the locomotive by the use of a bogie.

This was not as radical as it might seem. Gresley was rightly famous for his use of articulated carriage sets and two ex-North Eastern Railway three-cylinder Atlantics of Class C7 (NER Class Z) were rebuilt with articulation in 1930 and were reclassified C9. In their case the bogie incorporated a booster — a small geared steam engine that could increase starting tractive effort and could be taken out of gear at about 30mph. The modification was to enable these otherwise excellent locomotives to accelerate heavy expresses from out-of-course stops such as those which could occur against adverse signals on the 1 in 96 of Cockburnspath bank between Dunbar and Berwick. It was hoped that such equipment would enable double-heading to be eliminated whilst using perfectly serviceable locomotives at a time when funds available for new locomotives were severely restricted.

In the event the boosters caused their own problems in both operating and maintenance, problems exacerbated by the introduction of 'common-user' manning of footplate crews. The booster equipment was therefore removed in 1936 and 1937 but in any case the spread of new Pacifics had removed the requirement for the locomotives to perform more exacting duties although the articulated bogies were retained until the engines were withdrawn during the war.

The 'improved K3' (briefly referred to as K4) was drawn up in 1931 and two examples were referred to in the 1932 building programme. Preliminary design work was carried out at Darlington before the project was transferred to Doncaster. A major problem was that the larger wheels meant a higher pitched boiler and thus squat boiler fittings and a short chimney which would almost certainly have resulted in poor visibility for the driver due to drifting exhaust. The project was eventually dropped and the two locomotives on order cancelled in October 1933, eight months before the first proposal for the V2 'proper'.

A wide-firebox 2-6-2 was drawn up in August 1934 and was very much a smaller version of the 2-8-2 No.2001 *Cock o' the North* which had been built in May 1934 and underwent many trials throughout the summer months. At a meeting of his area mechanical engineers and the locomotive running superintendents on 3rd October 1934 held in the boardroom at King's Cross, Gresley revealed the proposal and the running superintendents "considered that this type of engine would be so much better for certain classes of work than the K3s and they wished to re-cast their proposals with a view to include some engines of this type".

Fourteen of the new locomotives — designated Class V2 — were provisionally earmarked for the 1935 building programme and the first five were ordered from Doncaster Works in May 1935. However, in August that year a new diagram was issued which eliminated most of the special features of *Cock o' the North* (rotary cam poppet valve gear and A.C.F.I. feed water heater) and showed a locomotive carrying a Bugatti-type streamlined casing similar to the new A4 class, No.2509 *Silver Link* of which was nearing completion in the Works at that time.

By October 1935 a diagram had been produced showing no streamlining whatsoever although a vee-fronted cab was retained, a feature which helped reduce reflections from the fire when running at night. Generally, the V2s continued the graceful lines of the A1 and A3 Pacifics but internally incorporated many of the improvements made to the Pacific design in the A4, including larger diameter piston valves and a longer combustion chamber in the firebox.

One feature made much of at the time was the casting of all three cylinders in one, a technique first begun at Doncaster in 1930 with Gresley's Class V1 2-6-2Ts. Whilst this would have been notable had the cylinders been cast in steel, they were only made in cast iron and such monobloc castings had been used by the North Eastern Railway in its three-cylinder designs since before the Great War, although the castings were supplied from the foundry of Kitson & Co. of Leeds who continued to be a supplier of various castings to the LNER. The monobloc concept was used on the V2s and the normal steam supply pipes to the outside cylinders were incorporated as

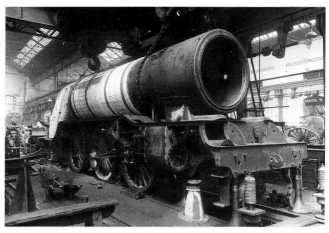

The very first V2, Green Arrow, *under construction at Doncaster in 1936. The boiler, having been lagged, is being lowered onto the chassis which has itself been lowered onto its driving wheels. The plain single blastpipe can be seen on the ground near the front footsteps which, incidentally, were left off the engine when completed and not fitted until later.* (LNER/Doncaster Official)

The large monobloc casting for all three cylinders of a V2 on a Stirk Hiloplane machine which is carrying out the operation of slotting the motion bar feet at Darlington Works in October 1947.
(LNER Official)

internal steam passages in the castings, making for a neat and pleasing appearance.

Unfortunately cast iron when damaged was very difficult to repair (at that time — there are newer techniques today) and complete castings had to be replaced whereas with separate cylinders there was no such problem. From 1956, therefore, when cylinders were in need of renewal separate castings were used and outside steam pipes supplied to the outside cylinders. Had steel castings been used repairs by welding, even quite major ones, would have been possible. Steel would also have been considerably lighter.

The only other significant design change in the lifetime of the V2s was the modification of the leading pony truck to spring control in place of the swing-link control originally fitted. These modifications came following several derailments involving V2s, usually on poor track, a legacy of heavy traffic and the lack of wartime maintenance. The laminated bearing springs of these trucks were also replaced by those of the helical type and for most of the class this work was carried out concurrently.

TABLE 2 — Locomotives built

| | BUILDER | | | |
| | Doncaster | | Darlington | |
Year	LNER Nos.	BR Nos.	LNER Nos.	BR Nos.
1936	4771-5	60800-4		
1937			4776-95	60805-24
1938			4796-4814	60825-43
1939	4843-6	60872-75	4815-42	60844-71
			4853-62	60882-91
1940	4847-52	60876-81	4863-88	60892-917
1941	3655-60	60928-33	4889-98	60918-27
1942	3661-4	60934-7	4899, 3641-54, 3665-74	60938-62
1943			3675-90	60963-78
1944			3691-5	60979-83

Notes: 3695 (BR No.60983) was the last engine built to Gresley's three-cylinder layout, in July 1944 and was withdrawn in September 1962. Between the original LNER numbers and the BR ones some engines carried a 1946 number and all carried a second 1946 number (i.e. the BR number less 60000).

TABLE 3 — Named engines

No.	Name	Date	Ceremony	Performed by
4771	*Green Arrow*	As built	No ceremony	——
4780	*The Snapper, The East Yorkshire Regiment, The Duke of York's Own*	11th Sept 1937	Hull Paragon Station	Brig-Gen. J. L. J. Clarke, Colonel of Regiment
4806	*The Green Howard, Alexandra, Princess of Wales's Own Yorkshire Regiment*	24th Sept 1938	Richmond Station	Maj-Gen. H. E. Franklyn, Colonel of Regiment
4818	*St. Peter's School, York, A.D. 627*	3rd April 1939	York Station	J. T. Brocklebank, Head Boy
4831	*Durham School*	15th June 1939	Durham Elvet Station	C. G. Ferguson, Head Boy
4843	*King's Own Yorkshire Light Infantry*	20th May 1939	Doncaster Works Yard	Lady Deedes, wife of Colonel of Regiment
4844	*Coldstreamer*	20th June 1939	King's Cross Station	Maj-Gen. Sir Cecil Pereira, deputising for Colonel of Regiment
60964	*The Durham Light Infantry*	29th April 1958	Durham Station	Col. K. M. W. Leather, Colonel of Regiment

A few of the V2s received double blastpipes and chimneys with the aim of improving draughting when burning the poorer quality coal prevalent for secondary duties in the 1950s and early 1960s. Two engines were fitted with the ex-LMSR 'Royal Scot' type and a further six with the French Kylchap arrangement, as fitted to the A4 and Peppercorn Pacifics. These alterations were made in 1960 and 1961 but came too late to affect the destiny of the class. During 1952 and 1953 No.60845 underwent a comprehensive testing programme at Swindon on the Western Region and in May 1953, following the Southern Region's temporary withdrawal of its Bulleid Pacifics, six V2s were transferred to Nine Elms shed from where they principally worked services between Waterloo and Bournemouth. The engines returned to their home sheds in June and July of that year.

All in all, the V2s were a very successful design, particularly as they survived on far less care and maintenance than did the Pacifics and yet were expected to stand in for the latter. That there were problems with the 2-to-1 valve gear is well known. Most of these were due to lack of maintenance and modifications were needed to keep out grit and ashes whilst still retaining accessibility. Gresley was aware of this and no doubt, had he not died at such an early age on 5th April 1941, would have found a solution.

Between 1936 and 1944 184 of the class were constructed, all but 25 of them at Darlington. They were employed throughout the LNER main line from London King's Cross to Edinburgh and Aberdeen, on the former Great Central main line from London Marylebone to Leicester, Sheffield and Manchester, on the Waverley route between Edinburgh and Carlisle and over the GN/GC line from Doncaster via Lincoln to March (although route restrictions precluded their use further into East Anglia. At the end of the LNER era in December 1947 V2s were distributed to the following depots: King's Cross, New England (Peterborough), Doncaster, Copley Hill (Leeds), York, Darlington, Gateshead, Heaton (Newcastle), Tweedmouth, Haymarket (Edinburgh), Dundee and Aberdeen Ferryhill. (Interestingly, none was based on the GC line at that time). The largest allocations were to be found at those sheds responsible for working important fast goods trains. Withdrawals began in February 1962 and by the beginning of 1966 only fourteen remained in service; the last one — No.60836 of Dundee — was withdrawn in December that year.

The 'Green Arrows' were primarily built for heavy fast freights and when the engines were in good condition were unsurpassed in their duties. The first five engines were distributed to King's Cross (No.4771), York (Nos.4772/3), New England, Peterborough (No.4774) and Dundee (No.4775). The class was soon able to show its paces on passenger trains, both booked turns and excursions and also when standing in for failed Pacifics on crack expresses and, occasionally, even the streamliners. During the Second World War the class was responsible for prodigious feats of haulage and after the ending of that conflict continued to be fully used in the heavy traffic on the ECML in the late 1940s and throughout the 1950s.

The V2s were big and heavy locomotives and thus were not capable of going 'anywhere' on the LNER system as, for instance, were the 'Black Fives' on the LMSR. However, any universal locomotive will be severely limited as to its axle load and weight per foot run and therefore as to its possible power. Whereas the V2s were shown to be capable of deputizing for Pacifics on the most arduous of express passenger turns, in similar circumstances on the West Coast Main Line 'Black Fives' would lose time. It is no surprise, then, to learn that Derby drawing office was preparing an equivalent to the V2 during the war years for possible post-war construction.

The success of the V2s led Gresley to look for a new design for the secondary routes and those over which the class was barred and produced a miniaturised version — the V4. Only two were built, Nos.3401-2 (BR Nos.61701-2), the first being named *Bantam Cock*. They were constructed in early 1941 and were capable of working 5,000 of the 6,414 route miles of the LNER whereas the V2s were limited to 2,752. Tragically Sir Nigel Gresley died shortly after delivery of No.3402 and no more were ordered, with the pair spending their working lives in Scotland.

Nobody who is familiar with the preserved *Green Arrow* can have an inkling of how run-down and poorly-maintained many of the class were during the 1940s and '50s. *Green Arrow* steams well, is very fast and rides like a coach. That is how they all should have been but often weren't in the real world of those days. Nevertheless the design was basically a very good one and, like its little brother *Bantam Cock*, deserved attention and possible improvement during the steam years of British Railways.

The LNER staged a number of exhibitions of locomotives and rolling stock during the 1930s with the proceeds going to charitable causes. No.4771 Green Arrow *was on display at New Barnet during an exhibition on 5th/6th June 1937 which attracted 16,000 visitors and raised £560 for railway and other charities.* (Colour-Rail NE28)

Right

Green Arrow *somewhat incongruously painted in BR lined black livery at Doncaster shed after a works overhaul in March 1954. The tender carries the first version of the BR totem.*
(J. Davenport/Colour-Rail BRE440)

A rare shot of two prototypes of their respective classes together at King's Cross depot on 16th September 1961. No.60800 Green Arrow *stands next to the first of the A4 Pacifics, No.60014* Silver Link, *which has the 'cod's mouth' of its streamlined frontage open for access to the smokebox. One of the early proposals for the V2 class would have had it adopt a streamlined form similar to the A4s.*
(R.C. Riley)

No.60847 (LNER No.4818) was named St. Peter's School, York A.D. 627 — *one of only eight named V2s — at a ceremony at that city's station on 3rd April 1939. It was allocated to York depot and, with the Minster in the background, is seen in not too clean a condition departing from its home city with a northbound express in September 1959. Note the neatly-tended bushes alongside the main line.* (P.J. Hughes/Colour-Rail BRE442)

The North British Railway's line between Edinburgh and Carlisle — the Waverley route — ran for some 98 miles through the sparseley-populated openness of the Lowlands and the Border Counties. The V2s were widely employed on this line where their haulage capacity, especially on freight traffic, was put to good use on its steep gradients. No.60813 heads an up mixed freight on the climb through Tynehead in April 1965. The closure of the Waverley route in January 1969 was one of the major closures of the post-Beeching era and left a vast area without rail connection.

(T.B. Owen/Colour-Rail SC281)

The V2s were the mainstay of fast freight working on the East Coast Main Line. Another of the 'namers' No.60835 The Green Howard, Alexandra, Princess of Wales's Own Yorkshire Regiment *(the longest of the V2 names!) is going well with a fitted freight at Drem in April 1961.*

(The late J.G. Wallace/Colour-Rail SC514)

No.60872 King's Own Yorkshire Light Infantry *nicely portrayed at York shed in September 1959. The regiment's name is perpetuated on a 'Deltic' diesel-electric locomotive preserved in the National Collection.*

(P.J. Hughes/Colour-Rail BRE443)

On the Waverley route again, No.60969 coasts through Stobs station, on the long descent from Whitrope Summit, with a partially-fitted Carlisle—Millerhill (Edinburgh) freight on a sunny evening on 20th July 1963. This locomotive was rebuilt with separate cylinders and outside steam pipes in 1960.

(J.S. Gilks/Colour-Rail SC740)

At the London end of the East Coast Main Line, No.60820 stands at Belle Isle, waiting to back down into King's Cross station c1960.

(Atlantic collection)

Left
The V2 class had a long association with the Great Central route from Marylebone to Nottingham, Sheffield and Manchester. Before the rundown of 'the last main line' in the 1960s, No.60831 calls at Lutterworth with a Marylebone—Nottingham Victoria service in July 1959. Most of the GC route was closed in 1966.

(G.H. Hunt/Colour-Rail BRE1356)

Another view of No.60831 which, two months after the above photograph, was transferred from Leicester to York with the rest of the GC shed's V2 allocation. It is seen here in the shed yard at York towards the end of its career, its paintwork shabby and peeling though at least valiantly cleaned. It had been rebuilt with separate cylinders in 1957 and became the penultimate V2 to be withdrawn from service, on 6th December 1966. (David Sutcliffe)

Green Arrow *ex-works on 1st June 1936 carrying its originally-allocated number and a curved nameplate. The brass works plate mounted on the smokebox was moved to the cabside below the number (4771) before the engine went into service.*

(LNER/Doncaster Official)

'A GREEN THOUGHT IN A GREEN SHADE'

On 21st February 1935 the Joint Locomotive & Traffic Committee of the LNER approved the construction of five of its new design of mixed traffic 2-6-2 engines — to be designated the V2 class. The previous November the Committee had resolved that its provisional programme for 1935 should consist of locomotives "of the general utility type, capable of hauling excursions, fish trains and fast braked freight trains". In deciding to commence construction of the V2s, it was equipping the railway with a class of locomotives which were to fulfil that specification and more.

On the pioneer member of the class was bestowed the name *Green Arrow*. As explained earlier in this book, the name was taken from that of the railways' fast registered goods service but its adoption on the first of the V2s was suggested by R.A. Thom, Mechanical Engineer at Doncaster; the inspiration apparently came to him whilst shaving one morning! The first five were initially planned to be numbered 637/9/40/64/70 but the allotted numbers were soon changed to 4771-5. *Green Arrow* was actually painted in photographic grey with the number 637 but was renumbered 4771 before entering service. When photographed as No.637, the locomotive carried a curved nameplate on the running board over the centre driving wheels but the now-familiar straight nameplates on the sides of the smokebox were provided before it was put into traffic in the LNER's eye-catching apple green livery.

No.4771's working life officially began with its allocation to King's Cross depot — the famous 'Top Shed' — on 22nd June 1936 but before going to London it was given ten days of running-in from Doncaster. These turns involved working the 6.16am local passenger train to Cleethorpes, then the 10.50 Cleethorpes—Barnetby, returning on the 11.44 from there to Doncaster. These were followed by slow trains on the Great Northern main line to Grantham and Peterborough, returning to Doncaster on the afternoon Harrogate express from King's Cross.

The locomotive worked up to London for the first time on 3rd July, hauling the 2.35pm semi-fast from Doncaster, and began an association with King's Cross which, apart from one brief interlude, was to remain steadfast throughout its career. The next day it was rostered to work the 11.30am York semi-fast as far as Grantham, returning with the first part of the so-called 'Junior Scotsman'.

The V2 swiftly established a favourable reputation for its mastery of everything demanded of it and *Green Arrow* became a particular favourite at 'Top Shed'. During its first few weeks there it was put to work in the Express Goods Link and regularly hauled the important 3.40pm fast freight from King's Cross to Glasgow as far as Peterborough, returning on an express fish train from Hull. During the summer No.4771 was also employed on East Coast Main Line passenger traffic to and from Peterborough, notably the 11.38am express from Leeds and Cleethorpes and the 5.30pm express from Leeds. On Saturday 25th July it was busily occupied working the 12.05pm to Grantham, returning to King's Cross with the 3.55 Scottish relief express, followed at 10.53 by the Leeds part of the 10.45 express.

Within its first few months in traffic, *Green Arrow* had succesfully performed all the sort of work envisaged for the V2 class and proved that the LNER had produced for itself an exceptional design of locomotive. On the 3.40pm Glasgow express goods it was recorded working 47 vehicles (610 tons gross) between Sandy and Peterborough in 38 minutes for the 32.3 miles, with a top speed of 66mph. On Christmas Eve 1936 a timer on the 1.05pm relief 'Midday Scotsman' (loaded to 455 tons), worked by No.4771 from King's Cross to Grantham, recorded a maximum speed of 86mph through Arlesey with 60 miles run at an average of 70.9mph. Impressive performances for a "general utility engine"!

The most important of the fast goods services from London was the 3.40pm down 'Scotch Goods'. Green Arrow *is seen here storming north near Marshmoor in 1937. Good permanent way maintenance was essential when a string of short-wheelbase wagons was hurried along at speeds of 60mph+. During and after the war derailments of such wagons became more frequent and, very much later, led to research which was to result in the theory behind the Advanced Passenger Train.* (NRM/LPC 23843)

I n a class of this size it is not easy to trace the career details of an individual locomotive. Whereas fellow members of the National Collection *Mallard* and *Duchess of Hamilton* belong to small classes of express locomotives employed on the most prestigious passenger work and had particularly illustrious careers (the former with its world speed record in 1938, the latter with its visit to the USA in 1939), *Green Arrow* was one of the 'workhorses' which earned the railway its 'daily bread'. In many ways, though, its status as a 'bread and butter' engine justifies its place in preservation ahead of some of the more glamorous candidates.

By the end of 1939 Britain was at war and the railways were facing difficult times as they took the strain of the war effort. Hard-pressed to meet the demands of moving munitions, war materials and troops, they had not the time, money or labour for any but the most essential maintenance. Fast freights were largely discontinued and the V2s found themselves on loose-coupled goods and coal trains. The class has earned the epithet "the engines that won the war"; that same description has been applied equally justifiably to other classes but the V2s undoubtedly performed some tremendous haulage feats during those dark days. For instance, on 31st March 1940 No.4800 was recorded leaving Peterborough with no fewer than 26 coaches (850 tons gross) on a King's Cross—Newcastle train.

With mechanical maintenance at a premium, the cleaning of paintwork was a luxury which could rarely be indulged in and LNER engines began to be turned out in a plain black livery. *Green Arrow* became a black locomotive in November 1941; the following February the abbreviated lettering 'N E' replaced the company's full initials on the tender as a further minor economy.

After the war the LNER implemented a complete renumbering scheme designed to give all members of a particular class a range of consecutive numbers instead of the previous random and anarchic numbering system. The first proposal of the scheme gave the V2s the numbers 700-883 and so *Green Arrow* became No.700 at the beginning of 1946. However, it had not actually carried that number before the renumbering of the V2s was changed to 800-983 and *Green Arrow* received its new number 800 on 12th November that year.

14

Apart from Green Arrow *only seven more V2s out of a total of 184 were ever named, although there is no doubt that had war not intervened more would have been so treated.* No.4780 The Snapper, The East Yorkshire Regiment, Duke of York's Own *is captured here following the naming ceremony on 11th September 1937 at Hull Paragon station when it was named by Brig-Gen. J.L.J. Clarke, Colonel of the Regiment, to commemorate the Coronation of HM King George VI who was Colonel-in-Chief of the East Yorkshire Regiment. The engine is backing on to the stock of the 5.00pm to King's Cross with which it departed shortly afterwards.*

(NRM/Real Photos 6105)

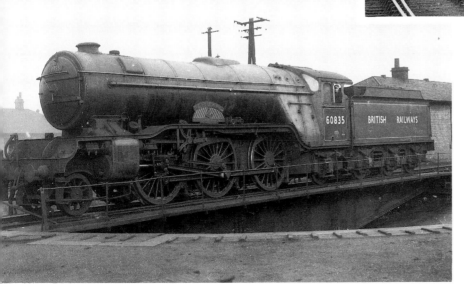

Above:
A typical pre-war scene on the East Coast route as No.4825 *hurries an up express through Sandy in 1939.* (NRM/LPC 23845)

Left
Repainting in BR livery may have been the first cleaning that many V2s had received since the 1940s decade began. No.60835 (originally No.4806 of September 1938) The Green Howard, Alexandra, Princess of Wales's Own Yorkshire Regiment *is seen here with the early type of lettering and in lined BR black. The tender carried is the earlier type of LNER standard and was originally coupled to D49 No.336.*

Above:
Notwithstanding that the train — 'The Scarborough Flyer' — supposedly has some prestige, the stock is a mixed bag and the locomotive absolutely filthy, hiding its identity. It is, in fact, No.60982, the penultimate engine of the class built at Darlington in June 1944 and surviving until October 1964. The location is Potters Bar and the date September 1951.
(NRM/LPC 24878)

The worst accident involving a V2 was the Balby Bridge collision at Doncaster on 9th August 1947 when No.936 (shown here), hauling a King's Cross—Leeds express, ran into the back of the 'Yorkshire Pullman'. Eighteen passengers were killed. (NRM/Doncaster Official 47/138)

Right:
No.813 (originally No.4784 of September 1937) was fitted with this stovepipe chimney and small smoke deflectors in December 1946. Although apparently successful, no more engines of the class were so fitted although this one retained its unique appearance until withdrawal in September 1966. The photograph was taken at King's Cross probably just prior to nationalization.
(NRM/C.C.B. Herbert)

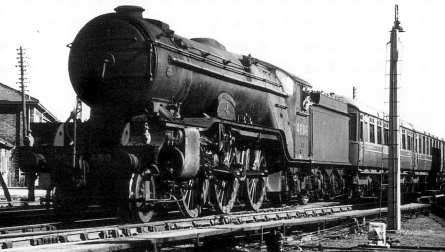

No.60963 at York shed in 1961 and as fitted with double blastpipe and chimney in February 1960. The blastpipe was based on the rebuilt 'Royal Scot' arrangement and was also fitted to No.60817. A further six V2s were fitted with double Kylchap arrangements.

(NRM/P. Ransome-Wallis XI 383)

Left:
Five V2s built in 1938 (Nos.4804-8) were equipped with 'MeLeSco' multiple-valve regulators, the control rodding for which can be seen along the boiler above the handrail on No.4806 The Green Howard *on a down express at Ripon. The gear was removed from all engines during the war and replaced by the standard arrangement, No.4806 being the last to be treated, in September 1944.*

(David V. Beeken)

In August 1948 the East Coast Main Line in Scotland between Berwick and Dunbar and many secondary routes in the Border Counties were badly hit by devastating floods which washed away bridges, embankments and track. On the ECML in the five miles between Grantshouse and Reston alone, seven bridges were swept away when the Eye Water burst its banks and it was the end of October before the route was re-opened. A year later a temporary structure is still in place, though new concrete abutments have been constructed, as V2 No.60801 eases across Bridge 123 near Grantshouse in August 1949.

(NRM/LPC 24875)

Lincoln's 12th century cathedral dominates the city and its railways as a clean No.60934 crosses the River Witham, west of Lincoln Central station, with a working over the GN/GE Joint Line in 1950. (NRM/P. Ransome-Wallis XI 365)

No.60869, steaming well and apparently leak-free, with an up fish train near Great Ponton in 1953. This, a New England (Peterborough) engine, typifies that depot's collection of V2s — absolutely filthy.

(NRM/P. Ransome-Wallis XI 368)

No.60819, in clean BR green livery and carrying the later style of totem, crosses the Forth Bridge in 1958 with an up express composed of BR standard Mk1 carriage stock. (NRM/LPC 23917)

Nationalization of the railways took effect on 1st January 1948 and *Green Arrow* duly passed into the ownership of the Eastern Region of British Railways. A further renumbering was necessary to unify all the locomotives of the new nationalized system and so 60000 was added to the existing numbers of the ex-LNER fleet. Application of the new numbers inevitably took some time to complete and *Green Arrow* did not actually receive its BR number 60800 until 4th February 1949.

With a new owner came a new livery — lined black in the style of the old London & North Western Railway which had been decided on, after a series of experiments, for mixed traffic locomotives. Repainting was generally carried out as locomotives passed through the works for overhaul and No.60800 emerged in this livery at the same time as it received its new number, following repairs at Doncaster. The name 'BRITISH RAILWAYS' was spelt out in full on the tender; the first version of the BR 'lion and wheel' emblem was not applied until the following November. (Ironically, considering the engine's name, it was actually in service painted black for longer than it was green!)

On 24th April 1953 Southern Region 'Merchant Navy' 4-6-2 No.35020 *Bibby Line* suffered a driving axle failure near Crewkerne whilst working a Waterloo—Exeter express and the whole class was withdrawn for examination. To assist with the SR's resultant motive power shortage, locomotives were loaned by other Regions with the Eastern contributing six V2s. Two more were sent to King's Cross to be held in reserve, including one from Leicester shed, and to provide cover on the Great Central line *Green Arrow* was temporarily transferred to Woodford Halse depot on 17th May. In the event, the Southern did not need the additional V2s and so No.60800 returned to King's Cross on 28th June; those six weeks were the only period the locomotive spent away from 'Top Shed'.

From 1956 separately-cast cylinders with outside steam pipes began to replace the V2s' original monobloc castings when new cylinders were required. *Green Arrow,* however, was to retain its monobloc cylinder casting until the end of its career, largely for reasons explained shortly. Also from the end

of that year the class started to be given the BR brunswick green livery, with orange and black lining, hitherto reserved for the principal express types. No.60800 entered Doncaster Works for overhaul in December 1957 and was turned out in its new livery on 11th January 1958 with the second version of the BR emblem on the tender. In November 1958 it received its final modification with the fitting of Automatic Warning System (AWS) equipment in line with the Ministry of Transport's recommendations following the Harrow collision in 1952.

Early in 1961 the British Transport Commission produced a list of historically-significant locomotives to be scheduled for official preservation and a place was set aside for *Green Arrow* on a number of grounds; it was the first large British high speed mixed traffic locomotive with a wide firebox and the prototype of the only 2-6-2 tender engine to go into series production. In fact, specific instructions were given that its monobloc cylinder casting was not to be replaced in order that it could be preserved in 'as built' condition.

The 1955 Modernization Plan had foreshadowed the demise of steam power on BR and with the increasing deployment of diesel traction on the East Coast Main Line in the early 1960s, the rundown of the steam fleet began to accelerate. Although the last examples would survive until the end of 1966, the first V2s were withdrawn in February 1962 as a result of a decision that any member of the class needing new cylinders would be scrapped and *Green Arrow* was to follow only six months later. It may be that a crack in the cylinder casting, which has required attention in recent years, prompted the decision to take it out of service but whatever the reason, the engine history card records that No.60800 was withdrawn from traffic on 21st August 1962. Unfortunately no final mileage is recorded.

From 1932 to 1962 (excepting the war years) a number of summer Saturday trains between Scotland or the North East of England and Scarborough avoided the congestion at York by being routed off the ECML at Pilmoor over a rural branch which meandered through Ryedale via Coxwold and Gilling to Malton where a double reversal was then needed to gain the Scarborough line. These trains continued long after the withdrawal of local services and a begrimed V2 No.60964 approaches the country junction at Gilling with a Scarborough—Glasgow working during the summer of 1957. The fireman has the single line token ready to exchange with the signalman.

(NRM/P.Ransome-Wallis XI 371)

Below:
V2s were truly mixed traffic locomotives and were often used on heavy, slow freight trains. No.60821 is seen here on an up coal train near Yaxley in 1953.

(NRM/P. Ransome-Wallis XI 370)

Gresley's 'mini' version of the V2 was the V4 of which only two were built, at a critical time in the war and only weeks before Sir Nigel's death in 1941. The first engine, No.3401 Bantam Cock, was exhibited at York on 11th February 1941 and undertook trials over various parts of the LNER system, being transferred to the Great Eastern section on 21st June 1941 and working from Stratford shed. Here, in August 1941, it is seen leaving Cambridge on the 11.04am express to Liverpool Street. (NRM/LPC 23842)

In BR days Bantam Cock was numbered 61700 and, with its sister engine No.61701, spent its working life in Scotland. In this illustration it is climbing out of Glasgow Queen Street (note the banker at the rear) on an Edinburgh-bound express. (NRM/LPC 23550)

Below:
Both V4s spent much of their lives allocated to Eastfield shed, Glasgow, and appeared occasionally on the West Highland line. Bantam Cock is captured here near Crianlarich in 1947 on a down goods train. The pair was withdrawn in 1957 after rather quiet lives and ended what could have been a much more useful design had BR developed it for quantity production. (NRM/P. Ransome-Wallis)

No.4771 Green Arrow *at King's Cross goods depot not long after entering service in 1936.* (NRM/C.C.B. Herbert)

A classic shot of Green Arrow *on the sort of duty for which it was built, pulling out of King's Cross goods yard with the 3.40pm express 'Scotch Goods' to Glasgow in 1936. Express freight it might have been, but short wheelbase four-wheel wagons were still the order of the day! An N2 0-6-2T and a GNR large Atlantic are awaiting a path to proceed to King's Cross passenger station.*

(NRM/C.C.B. Herbert)

A superb study of Green Arrow *at the head of a King's Cross—Leeds express near Potters Bar in 1949. The locomotive has not long been repainted in the new BR lined black livery, as No.60800, with 'BRITISH RAILWAYS' in full on the tender.*

(NRM/P.Ransome-Wallis XI 364)

THE WEARING OF THE GREEN IN THE NATIONAL COLLECTION

On being withdrawn from service at King's Cross, *Green Arrow* passed into the custody of the BTC's Curator of Historical Relics (the term 'National Collection' did not really come into use until the transfer of exhibits to the National Railway Museum in 1975) but despite the assurance of a place in preservation, a decade of uncertainty was to follow.

There was a promising start, however, with the locomotive being sent to Doncaster Works for restoration to exhibition standard. In fact, though an operational future was not envisaged in those days, restoration involved more than just a coat of paint and whilst at Doncaster *Green Arrow* was given a replacement boiler — one of 1944 construction previously carried by Nos.60825 and 60841. With the locomotive remaining substantially — and certainly superficially — as built, it was an easy decision to restore it to its LNER condition and livery and in April 1963 *Green Arrow* emerged from the paintshop resplendent in the company's distinctive apple green, with its original number 4771.

But there No.4771's preservation career rather came to a halt. The opening of the Museum of British Transport at Clapham in 1963 provided a home for a good many of the historic exhibits owned by the British Railways Board (which succeeded the BTC that year) but all the available space had been allocated and for *Green Arrow* (and others) it was "no room at the inn". For over a year No.4771 was stored in the Doncaster paintshop (during which time a transfer to the care of Doncaster Corporation was mooted) but in October 1964 it was moved to the closed locomotive shed at Hellifield which was being used to accommodate some of the homeless preserved BRB collection.

1967 saw *Green Arrow* on the move again, this time to Leicester where a possible home for several of the BRB locomotives had been proposed in a Museum of Technology but it was a plan which ultimately came to nought. No.4771 lan-

Bill Harvey, architect of No.4771's return to steam, checks the washout plugs during the steam test at Norwich. (Dr. W.J. Naunton)

guished in the old Midland locoshed until 1970 but, with the demolition of the building, it was time to move on again and in September the engine was transferred to the old Pullman car shops at Preston Park, Brighton, which had become the depository for stored exhibits. Things, however, were about to change for the better.

The graceful lines of the V2 class can be seen to originate with Gresley's earlier A1/A3 Pacifics in this view of No.4771 and the renowned A3 No.4472 Flying Scotsman *heading through the Aire Valley at Crosshills with a train of privately-owned vehicles on 13th September 1975.* (John S. Whiteley)

Bringing steam back to the Settle & Carlisle line, No.4771 storms past Mallerstang on the climb towards Ais Gill Summit with the first southbound run on 27th March 1978. (David Eatwell)

In October 1971 the National Collection-owned GWR 4-6-0 No.6000 *King George V* became the first locomotive to breach a ban on steam on BR lines which had been enforced since the end of steam traction in 1968. Its successful tour prompted a gradual opening of the railway system to steam-hauled special trains and some people began to think that *Green Arrow* might have a part to play in the action.

One of them was D.W. (Bill) Harvey, shedmaster at Norwich and master craftsman of steam. He had seen No.4771 during its doldrum period at Leicester and Preston Park and suggested that the engine could be restored to working order at his depot where he would have the assistance of members of the Norfolk Railway Society. Towards the end of 1971 agreement was reached with the BRB for No.4771 to be overhauled at Norwich — provided it incurred no expense other than its movement! — and so on the night of 20th/21st January 1972 the locomotive was hauled from Brighton via Redhill, Clapham Junction, Dalston, Temple Mills and Bishops Stortford.

Over the next twelve months *Green Arrow* was thoroughly examined and carefully prepared for steaming and there is no doubt that Bill Harvey's meticulous attention in 1972/3 (especially to the valve gear) has stood the locomotive in good stead ever since. On 12th August 1972 No.4771 was steamed for the first time in almost ten years and on 28th March 1973 made a succesful trial run to Ely and back. *Green Arrow* was at last ready to return to the public stage and on 5th April it left Norwich to run in steam via Peterborough and Leicester to the Birmingham Railway Museum at Tyseley where it was the star attraction at an open weekend on 2nd/3rd June.

Green Arrow re-entered main line service on 10th June 1973 hauling three trains between Birmingham Moor Street and Stratford-upon-Avon over the North Warwickshire line, followed on 1st July by two specials between Tyseley and Didcot in conjunction (appropriately) with A4 Pacific No.4498 *Sir Nigel Gresley*. The next day the two engines travelled together via Derby and Leeds to Carnforth, where the Steamtown Railway Museum was to be No.4771's base for the next couple of years.

The locomotive worked a number of excursions from Carnforth over the Cumbrian Coast line and via Skipton to Leeds during its time at Steamtown but in 1975 there came another change in its fortunes with the opening of the new National Railway Museum in York which was to be its future home. That year also saw the celebration of the 150th anniversary of the Stockton & Darlington Railway, the first public railway in the world to employ steam locomotives. The climax of an extensive programme of events was a grand cavalcade of locomotives at Shildon and No.4771 therefore travelled to the north east to participate in the parade on 31st August. On 27th September the NRM was opened by HRH The Duke of Edinburgh and *Green Arrow* was in steam for the occasion, with the Duke enjoying a visit to the footplate and briefly taking the controls. The NRM had been established as part of the Science Museum and with its founding the National Collection passed into the custodianship of the Department of Education & Science (as it then was; today the Department of Culture, Media & Sport) as the culmination of the provisions of the 1968 Transport Act.

A pause in No.4771's activities then ensued, with a boiler retube required before their resumption. This was carried out at York by contractors in 1977 and the engine returned to steam that August, following which it was given a full repaint. The main line steam programme, meanwhile, had continued to expand and a major development in 1978 was the long-awaited re-opening to steam of the Settle & Carlisle line. *Green Arrow* was chosen to haul the first specials on this classic route over the Easter weekend. The locomotive ran with a 'Norfolkman' headboard, a strange title for a train running through the Pennine hills, perhaps, but a well-merited tribute to Bill Harvey who had made such a contribution to the preservation movement and the V2 in particular.

1978 was also notable for being the year in which BR ran its own steam-hauled services for the first time since 1968. In fact, two separate programmes were operated during the summer, one based on Carnforth and the Cumbrian Coast, the other running from York. The latter itinerary was over the York—Leeds—Harrogate—York circuit and No.4771 hauled the inaugural train on 25th June.

In 1979 the NRM marked the centenary of dining cars by running a train of restored catering vehicles on an extensive tour of the railway system during the course of which passengers were able to travel in the coaches and dine in style. Diesel traction was used for the majority of the tour but on the train's return to York the final flourish was a steam-hauled trip round the Harrogate 'circle' behind *Green Arrow* on 29th September — perhaps the NRM's crowning achievement as a working museum. That reputation as a live museum was amply demonstrated in 1980, the year in which the 150th anniversary of the Liverpool & Manchester Railway (the world's first steam-worked public passenger railway) was celebrated. Inspired by the Shildon event in 1975, another cavalcade of locomotives was arranged, this time over the three days of the May Bank Holiday weekend, at Rainhill where *Rocket* had triumphed in the 'Rainhill Trials' in 1829. No fewer than ten NRM locomotives participated in the parades, including *Green Arrow* which ran coupled to the Museum's restored LNER buffet car and East Coast Joint Stock brake van.

The centenary of catering on railways was celebrated in style in 1979 by a exhibition tour of restored NRM carriages. Green Arrow *is shown here on the last day of the tour leaving Leeds whilst taking the train round the Harrogate 'circle' on 29th September. The vehicles are LNWR Royal Brake No.5154, LNWR Royal Dining Car No.76, MR Dining Car No.3463, a BR MkI kitchen car, Pullman Cars* Emerald, Eagle *and* Topaz, *LNER Buffet Car No.9135, BR Griddle Car No.Sc1100 and LNWR Royal Brake No.5155 bringing up the rear.* (John S. Whiteley)

Two National Collection locomotives share haulage of a railtour from Leeds to Carnforth as Midland Railway Compound 4-4-0 No.1000 and Green Arrow *make an unlikely pairing in the cutting near Horsforth on 3rd May 1980.* (John S. Whiteley)

Below:
No.4771 leaves Totley Tunnel, the second longest in Britain, and runs into Grindleford whilst working from Sheffield to Manchester via the Hope Valley line on 9th November 1985.
(Les Nixon)

Another boiler retube was undertaken in 1984/5 by the Humberside Locomotive Preservation Group at its depot in Hull and No.4771 returned to service on the Harrogate 'circle' section of the 'Scarborough Spa Express' on 25th August, followed on 7th November by a trip to Manchester taking in the Hope Valley and Standedge routes.

One of the engine's most unusual assignments occurred on 7th April 1986 when EMI Music Ltd. chartered a special train from King's Cross to Gleneagles in connection with a corporate event at the famous Gleneagles Hotel and arranged for not only *Green Arrow* but also BR 2-10-0 No.92220 *Evening Star* to double-head the charter from Edinburgh. After working up the East Coast Main Line overnight, the pair duly worked the special to Gleneagles, ran forward to Perth for turning, then returned to Edinburgh before heading back south in the early hours of the 8th. *Evening Star* was detached at Darlington for a visit to the North Yorkshire Moors Railway and *Green Arrow* ploughed on homewards, only to be delayed for over an hour near Thirsk while the fire brigade attended to a suspected leak on a train of chemical tankers ahead! When No.4771 finally arrived back at the NRM, it had covered 550 miles of which only 54 had been spent actually hauling a train!

That may well have been its first visit to Scotland but the locomotive returned north of the border in 1987, visiting Dundee for the centenary of the second Tay Bridge on 20th June and then heading a special to Edinburgh over both the Tay and Forth Bridges. The following month saw *Green Arrow* back in London, spending five weeks at Marylebone during which time it worked several of the popular 'Sunday Lunch' excursions to Stratford-upon-Avon.

Strangely, having been the locomotive which brought steam back to the Settle—Carlisle line, No.4771 had to wait until February 1989 before it ventured into the Cumbrian mountains again but over the next four years it became quite a regular sight on this most demanding of routes, never failing to impress on its climbs to Ais Gill Summit, the highest main line summit in England. 1991 found it blazing a new trail for the V2 class far from its usual haunts when it visited Crewe during the summer and hauled a series of the BR-sponsored 'North Wales Coast Express' trains via Chester to Holyhead, earning the respect of footplatemen brought up on engines from the rival LMS camp.

With *Green Arrow's* current seven-year boiler certificate due to expire in 1992, it appeared that it might be the end of the line — for the foreseeable future, at least — for this most consistently reliable and popular of main line performers. No.4771's last run was from Carlisle to Bradford Forster Square on 1st August, accomplished with its customary syncopated style. After turning on the Shipley triangle, it slipped quietly back to York with the NRM support coach and made a farewell appearance in steam at a working weekend in the Museum yard on 5th/6th September.

The railways through the Pennines have proved to be amongst the most popular for steam specials and certainly provide some of the most scenic photographic opportunities. The mountains and fells of the Settle & Carlisle line are very different from the flat countryside of the East Coast Main Line but Green Arrow *is master of its task as it approaches Shotlock Hill Tunnel after surmounting the climb to Ais Gill on 1st May 1989.* (John S. Whiteley)

The terraced streets of the small Derbyshire town of New Mills provide a backcloth as No.4771 crosses the viaduct over the River Goyt during a run over the Hope Valley line on 26th April 1986.

(John S. Whiteley)

Many of Green Arrow's *travels in preservation have taken it over unusual routes for a V2. Here is the locomotive working hard on 26th April 1986 approaching Greenfield, with its distant signal at 'clear', on the ex-LNWR Standedge route amidst characteristic Pennine scenery in the Tame Valley. In the background are the chimneys and cooling towers of Hartshead power station.*

(Les Nixon)

28

A fine portrait of No.60800 Green Arrow, *in its final BR green livery, at Grantham with an up express to King's Cross in August 1961. It is this livery which has been adopted for the locomotive following its latest overhaul.*

(K.R. Pirt/Colour-Rail BRE798)

Green Arrow *in LNER apple green livery as No.4771 at Darlington Bank Top on 5th July 1987 with a special marking the station's centenary. The train travelled via Stockton and Leamside to Newcastle, then on to Hexham, returning over the East Coast Main Line.* (Michael Rutherford)

Against a backdrop of Black Combe, Green Arrow *passes Whitbeck crossing with a thirteen-coach special train over the Cumbrian Coast line from Carnforth to Ravenglass and Sellafield on 21st September 1974.* (J.S. Gilks)

No.4771 bursts out of the short Wescoe Hill Tunnel, near Weeton, with a BR-sponsored York—Leeds—Harrogate—York circular tour on 3rd September 1978. Steam excursions today use dedicated sets of privately-owned rolling stock generally painted in traditional colours but at the time of the last two photographs BR coaches in the then-standard blue and grey livery were utilised. They made an uneasy match with steam locomotive liveries!

(Hugh Ballantyne)

Springtime on the Settle & Carlisle line at Keld, just south of Long Marton, as No.4771 heads south into the Pennines on 1st May 1989. The garish mixture of carriage liveries — BR crimson lake, Pullman and InterCity — gives the train a rather inharmonious look but for the satisfaction of seeing steam in action on England's highest main line perhaps most things can be excused!

(John Shuttleworth)

The construction of the railway out of Chester involved some heavy engineering through tunnels and sandstone cuttings. Viewed from an unusual elevated vantage point, Green Arrow *emerges into the summer sunshine with the 'North Wales Coast Express' to Holyhead on 18th August 1991.*

(John Shuttleworth)

From the late 1970s to the early 1990s BR was widely involved in promoting steam-hauled excursions. In the late 1980s it organised a series of 'Sunday Lunch' specials with full dining facilities between Marylebone and Stratford-upon-Avon. In July 1987 Green Arrow *became the third NRM engine to participate in these workings and is seen well-cleaned outside the former Marylebone carriage shed, by then a diesel-unit depot.* (Michael Rutherford)

Right
For several years in the 1980s the 'Scarborough Spa Express' was a feature of the York railway scene during the summer months and was aimed at providing inexpensive steam trips for the family market. On 27th July 1986 No.4771 backs out of Scarborough station towards the turntable which was reinstated there especially for these trains in 1981. The locomotive was first recorded as visiting Scarborough with an excursion from King's Cross on Whit Sunday 1961. (Graham Maple)

Left
A V2 far from home on the North Wales Coast line. From 1989-92 BR organised a programme of trains, also aimed at the holiday market, from Crewe and Chester to Holyhead, calling at the main resorts along the coast. Green Arrow *departs from Rhyl, past the tall LNWR signal box (then disused), on 20th August 1991.* (Keith Jackson)

Super-power for the 'EMI Music Express' on 7th April 1986. Green Arrow *and BR Class 9F 2-10-0 No.92220* Evening Star *provide more than enough haulage as they double-head the private charter train over the Caledonian main line at Blackford en* route *from Edinburgh to Gleneagles.*
(John S. Whiteley)

The V2 worked a series of 'wine and dine' excursions between London Marylebone and Stratford-upon-Avon during the summer of 1987 and the locomotive is seen approaching Banbury on the return journey on 2nd August. The wide bridge is indicative of 'rationalised' trackwork — lines leading to the one-time Banbury hump yard formerly occupied the empty trackbed on the right. (Keith Jackson)

One of the factors which had enabled steam to return to Marylebone in 1985 was the survival of a turntable at the station. No.4771 is being turned on the vacuum-operated table during its 1987 visit to London. Note the sacks of coal on the back of the tender — in the absence of traditional servicing facilities, steam operations on the main line today have to be as self-contained as possible.

Below:
A V2 at Marylebone again, recalling Great Central route expresses of the late 1930s. Green Arrow has just arrived at the terminus from York on 18th July 1987.

The flats of Lisson Green Estate on the site of the former Marylebone goods depot overlook Green Arrow *as it departs past the diesel unit fuelling point with a Stratford-upon-Avon special on 26th July 1987.* (Keith Jackson)

Green Arrow *attacks the climb out of Stratford-upon-Avon returning to London on 2nd August 1987. The train is formed of BR MkI first class carriages in the then-current Inter-City livery. The semaphore signals are of interest; a Western Region lower quadrant gives a clear road for an incoming train, while the V2 proceeds under the authority of a later London Midland Region upper quadrant.* (Keith Jackson)

Green Arrow *climbs the bank out of Pontefract with a thirteen-coach special from York via Sheffield to Dinting for a visit to the now-closed Dinting Railway Centre (near Glossop) on 21st April 1979. In the background can be seen Ferrybridge power station.* (David Eatwell)

Green Arrow *rounds the curve off the Tay Bridge with a special marking its centenary on 20th June 1987. The Tay Bridge, at 2 miles 1,093 yards, is Europe's longest railway bridge and can be seen curving away to the right in the distance into Dundee.* (Les Nixon)